501

HORRIBLE BUT True

THINGS YOU'D RATHER NOT KNOW!

Written by
Helena Ramsay and Sandy Ransford

Vineyard BOOKS

ACKNOWLEDGMENTS

Picture credits
Abbreviations
AOL   Andromeda Oxford Limited
MEPL   Mary Evans Picture Library
RF   Rex Features

6tr I. Took/Biofotos; 7tr C. Roessler/Oxford Scientific Films; 14-15 Corbis-Bettmann/Reuter; 15tr Peter Brooker/RF; 17br Peter Newark's Historical Pictures; 18cl Sipa Press/RF; 18tr RF; 18br Frilet/Sipa Press/RF; 19br MEPL; 22 Popperfoto x2; 25t MEPL; 25bl Corbis-Bettmann/UPI; 26tl Popperfoto; 27tr Science Photo Library; 32tl Peter Newark's Historical Pictures; 32tr NASA; 33cr MEPL; 34tl MEPL; 34cl Hulton Getty; 40tl & tr Hulton Getty; 40br Popperfoto; 41t Peter Newark's Military Pictures; 44c Mourelle/Sipa Press/RF; 45tl Popperfoto; 45tr RF

Planned and produced by
Andromeda Oxford Limited
11–13 The Vineyard
Abingdon
Oxon OX14 3PX

Published in 1999 by
Bookmart Limited
Desford Road
Enderby
Leicester
LE9 5AD

ISBN 1-86199-004-9

Printed in Singapore

Contents

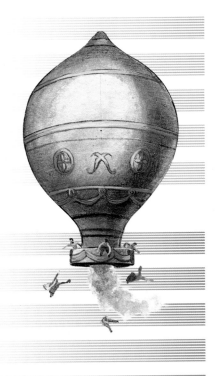

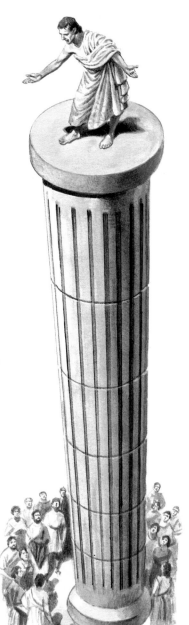

Dangerous Waters

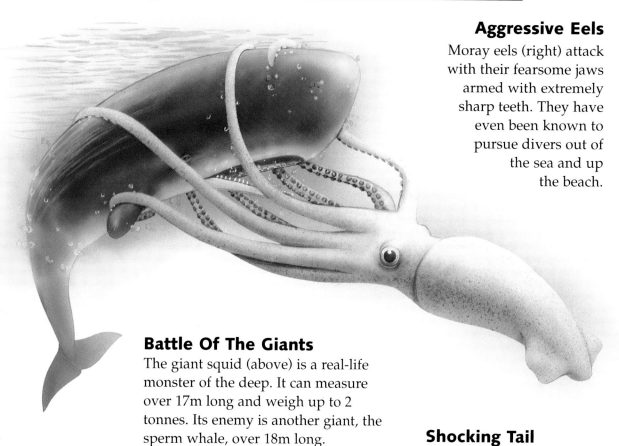

Aggressive Eels

Moray eels (right) attack with their fearsome jaws armed with extremely sharp teeth. They have even been known to pursue divers out of the sea and up the beach.

Battle Of The Giants

The giant squid (above) is a real-life monster of the deep. It can measure over 17m long and weigh up to 2 tonnes. Its enemy is another giant, the sperm whale, over 18m long. Legendary sea monsters that attacked ships are believed in many cases to have been giant squids.

Shocking Tail

Electric eels have been known to deliver electric shocks of up to 550 volts.

Living Spears

Needle fish live in tropical seas and oceans. Up to 1.5m long yet weighing only 4kg, these slender fish leap from the water when disturbed. It is bad news if someone gets in their way. One sailor was speared to his boat when a needle fish ran him through the leg.

Just When You Thought It Was Safe...

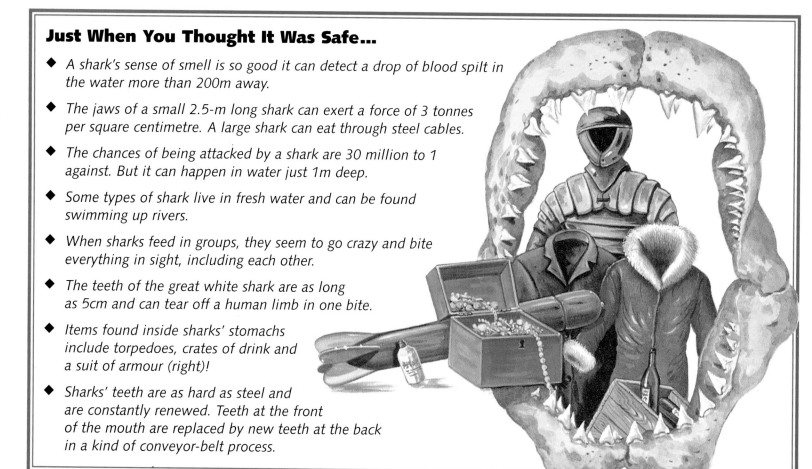

◆ A shark's sense of smell is so good it can detect a drop of blood spilt in the water more than 200m away.

◆ The jaws of a small 2.5-m long shark can exert a force of 3 tonnes per square centimetre. A large shark can eat through steel cables.

◆ The chances of being attacked by a shark are 30 million to 1 against. But it can happen in water just 1m deep.

◆ Some types of shark live in fresh water and can be found swimming up rivers.

◆ When sharks feed in groups, they seem to go crazy and bite everything in sight, including each other.

◆ The teeth of the great white shark are as long as 5cm and can tear off a human limb in one bite.

◆ Items found inside sharks' stomachs include torpedoes, crates of drink and a suit of armour (right)!

◆ Sharks' teeth are as hard as steel and are constantly renewed. Teeth at the front of the mouth are replaced by new teeth at the back in a kind of conveyor-belt process.

Fatal Poison

Grave Stones

Stonefish (right) are the most poisonous fish in the world. They look like stones or coral, but touch their spines and you will receive an injection of deadly venom.

Sea Stingers

The sea wasp, also known as the Australian box jellyfish, is the world's most venomous animal. It is known to have caused the death of at least 70 people in the last 100 years. Its poison attacks the heart, bringing death within 3 minutes of being stung if the victim is not given medical attention.

Killer Snails

Cone shells (right) possess fatal stings. They often have beautiful shells, and many victims have been divers who have picked them up to admire them.

Armed To Kill

The tentacles of the Portuguese man-of-war are extremely venomous. For humans, a bad sting means severe pain, a drop in blood pressure, and sometimes death.

Poison Puffer

The puffer fish is so called because it blows itself up with air or water in self defence. Its body contains a poison that can kill anyone who eats it within 24 hours, and so far there is no known antidote.

Piranha Horror

On 19 September 1981 more than 300 people were eaten alive by piranhas when a ferry capsized as it was docking at the Brazilian port of Obidos. Only 128 people survived.

Hypnotic Hunter

As a cuttlefish approaches its prey, its body becomes a kaleidoscope of changing colours and patterns. This mesmerises the prey and allows the cuttlefish to shoot out its tentacles and grab it.

Croc Attack

Lurking unseen in the river, a crocodile (right) swims silently towards its unsuspecting prey which, like this zebra, may have come to drink. It then launches itself out of the water, grabs its prey and tears off lumps of flesh.

Table Manners

❖

When eating a mussel or an oyster, a starfish pulls its victim's shell open. It then pushes its stomach into the shell, wraps it round its prey and digests it.

❖

The giant blue whale, over 30m long and weighing nearly 200 tonnes, eats only tiny shrimp-like creatures called krill, but it takes in millions at one mouthful.

❖

Crocodiles kill about 2000 people each year.

❖

If an octopus becomes upset, it may eat itself.

Insect Traits

Ants milk aphids for their honeydew. In return, the ants protect the aphids' eggs from predators.

Chasing victims at a speed of 60cm per second, the tiger beetle is the fastest insect in the world.

❖

The assassin bug pounces on unwary insects and then feeds by sucking out their body tissues.

Protection Racket

Puffin Power
Puffins avoid attack by wheeling through the sky in large groups when entering and leaving their nesting sites.

Back To Front
With false antennae on their wings, hairstreak butterflies fool their predators by flying away in an unexpected direction.

Leaving A Tail
The bright blue tail of the Californian skink attracts predators. If it is attacked the skink can detach its tail and leave it, still wriggling, with the predator.

Fighting Fit
If the pussmoth caterpillar is attacked, it squirts formic acid from blood-red filaments in its tail.

Deadly Frogs
1/100,000th of a gram of skin gland secretion of the arrow-poison frog (above) can kill a human.

Totally Repellent
The skunk (left) can squirt its horrible, protective scent up to 18m.

Fish Fishing
The batfish (below) hides from its prey by digging backwards into the sand. Propped up on its pelvic fins, it waits for its prey with only its front end protruding.

Tail Trap
The Australian death adder is a cunning creature. Perfectly camouflaged, it lies in wait for its prey with only the pink tip of its tail visible. By wriggling its tail tip to resemble a worm, it attracts hungry birds and then devours them.

Fast Food
A pair of swifts swooping through the skies can catch up to 20,000 insects in a single day.

Cowboy Spider
The bolas spider spins a single weighted thread, whirls it around its head and lassoes its insect prey.

Monkey Hunt
Generally content with fruit and leaves, chimpanzees occasionally hunt and eat monkeys. One chimp drives the monkeys towards another chimp, while others block their escape. When the unlucky victims discover they are ambushed they turn back and are immediately caught and killed by the hunters.

Nightmare Bat
The vampire bat preys on sleeping mammals such as cows or even humans. Settling gently so as not to wake its victim, it inserts razor-sharp teeth into the skin. The bat then laps blood from the wound.

Moving Target
Impala confuse their predators by running in different directions. As the herd scatters, hundreds of moving targets confuse the predator. Each impala springs into the air, leaping as high as 3m.

Champion Mouser

There was once a female cat called Towser which lived in a Scottish whisky distillery. Renowned as a mouser, it was estimated she had caught almost 29,000 mice in her 24 years of life. That is an average of over 3 a day.

Pelican Ring

Pelicans often fish together. Having formed a ring, they all dip their heads into the water at the same time. Fish within the ring may escape from one pelican's bill, only to be swallowed by another one (below).

Flower Power

The Malaysian orchid mantis looks like a beautiful white orchid. Unsuspecting insects in search of nectar are swiftly devoured.

Egg Box

Goal!

The kusimanse, an African dwarf mongoose, would play rugby well. It breaks eggs by picking them up in its forefeet and throwing them backwards between its splayed hindlegs. The egg inevitably hits something, cracks, and is eaten by the mongoose.

Spiked!

The African egg-eating snake is able to take whole eggs into its mouth. As it swallows, its spiked vertebrae slit the eggshell, allowing it to drink the yolk.

Smashing Time

When an Egyptian vulture (left) finds a clutch of ostrich eggs, it picks up stones and hurls them at the nest. Sooner or later it succeeds in smashing an egg, and then eats the contents.

Crushing Snake

The egg-eating snake of Africa swallows eggs whole, and has special bones in its throat to crush them.

Dead Dodo

When pigs and rats were brought to Mauritius in the 16th century, they hastened the extinction of the dodo by plundering the birds' nests.

Soldiering On

Some South American ants hunt in armies of 750,000. The soldier ants sometimes link legs to form a 'roof' protecting worker ants from the heat.

Heron Lure

Some herons in Japan pick up insects and cast them on water. Fish rising to the bait are then speared by the herons' sharp beaks.

Surf-riding

Sea-lion pups on the beaches of Patagonia are prey to killer whales (left). The whales surf in on a wave, grab a pup and catch the next wave out to sea again, without being stranded on the shore.

Weird Plants

Fast And Slow

Slow Grower

Puya raimondii, *at over 7m tall, is the largest of all herbs. Taking between 80 and 150 years to flower for the first time, it is also the slowest plant to produce flowers.*

Shooting Up

Some species of bamboo may grow nearly 1m in only 24 hours.

Noisy Flower

The flowers of the evening primrose (right) open at dusk. Their opening takes place so swiftly that it can both be seen and heard, as the buds burst open.

Chemical Weapons

A mature oak tree may have as many as 300 different species of insect living on it. The tree resists their attack with chemicals stored in its leaves (right) and bark.

Desert Plants

Plants that grow in deserts where it is extremely hot and dry have to guard against losing too much water. They do this by having few pores in their leaves or by having leaves protected by a waxy waterproof layer.

Big And Smelly

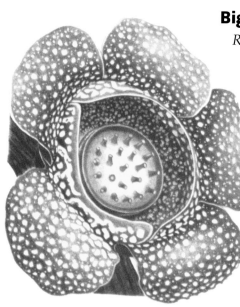

Rafflesia arnoldii (left) of West Sumatra is a foul-smelling parasitic plant. Its gigantic flowers can measure as much as 90cm across and an individual flower can weigh up to 7kg.

Slow And Sweet

The flowers of the South American *Heliconia* mature in sequence. Each flower releases only a drop of nectar at a time, forcing the hummingbirds that pollinate it to make repeated visits.

Ancient Algae

Blue-green algae discovered in fossil deposits at least 3.4 billion years old are identical to forms of blue-green algae living today.

Root Crop

One winter rye plant can produce 622.8km of roots in only 0.051cu m of soil. A member of the grass family, winter rye thrives in northern Europe.

Short Of Breath

Mangroves (left) grow on tropical coasts and in muddy swamps. The mud in which they grow contains only minute quantities of oxygen and the plants are regularly submerged at high tide. As a result, their roots have developed into knobbly tubes extending upwards into the air.

*It is thought that the
giant sequoia could last
forever were it not for the
fact that its wood is so
brittle that it eventually
cracks and falls.*

*The birthwort flower
looks like meat and
smells like rotting fish,
which makes it
attractive to flies that
help to pollinate it.*

*The foxglove and other
plants produce poisons
to prevent insects and
other animals from
eating them.*

❖

*The wild hairy potato
protects itself from
aphids by producing a
substance that imitates
their alarm scent.*

Meat-eating Plants

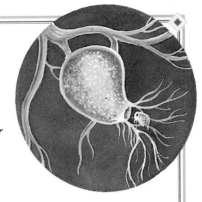

Bladderwort

As the bladders on the leaves of this floating plant
(right) open and water is drawn in, insects such as water
fleas and mosquito larvae are sucked in and consumed.

No Escape

The scaly insides of the
pitcher plant prevent
insects climbing out once
they have fallen in.

Venus Flytrap

The hinged leaves of the Venus flytrap are armed with
sensitive trigger hairs. When these are touched by an
insect, the two parts of the leaf snap together and the
spiked edges form a barred cage to trap the victim.

Crocus Corms

Crocuses store food in thickened, underground
stems known as corms. Each year the crocus grows
a new corm above the old one. To remain deep in
the soil, it has special roots that shorten, pulling the
corms downwards.

Ancient Seeds

Scientists have
discovered that seeds
from the oriental lotus
plant have germinated
some 3000 years after
their dispersal.

Green Giants

♦ The giant kelp seaweed can grow
45cm in a single day.

♦ The roots of the South African wild
fig tree can extend to a depth
of around 120m.

♦ The largest seed is that of the giant fan palm or coco-de-
mer that grows only in the Seychelles. The seed can weigh
up to 20kg.

♦ The leaves of the raffia palm, one of over 2500 species of
palm trees, are the largest in the world, growing to 20m in
length. Their leaf stalks, or petioles, alone can extend to
almost 4m.

♦ The world record for the weight of an onion stands at
5.55kg. This is heavier than a man's head.

♦ The banyan or Indian fig tree (right) produces shoots from
its vast spreading branches that take root to form new
trunks. The largest known specimen has some 1775
supporting roots and its canopy covers more than 1.2ha.

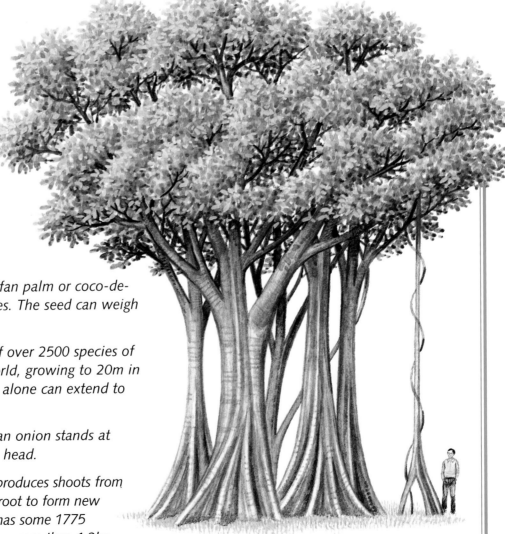

Prehistoric Life

Dinosaurs

Bighead!

The skull and neck frill of Torosaurus or 'piercing lizard' were over 2m long and weighed 2 tonnes.

Nutcase

Stegosaurus weighed 4 tonnes, but its brain was about the size of a walnut.

Fast Mover

Not all dinosaurs were slow. Dromiceiomimus or 'emu-mimic lizard', which lived in what is now Canada, could probably run faster than 60kph.

Tiny Dino

We think of dinosaurs as being huge, but the earliest were agile creatures only about 1m long.

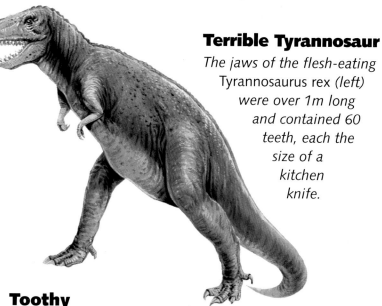

Toothy

Some of the duck-billed dinosaurs had as many as 2000 teeth in their beak-shaped jaws.

Long Lizard

The longest dinosaurs were the diplodocids. Seismosaurus, the longest yet discovered, was 40m in length.

Terrible Tyrannosaur

The jaws of the flesh-eating Tyrannosaurus rex (left) were over 1m long and contained 60 teeth, each the size of a kitchen knife.

Heavyweights

Some dinosaurs (the titanosaurids and the brachiosaurids) are estimated to have weighed up to 120 tonnes. This is the greatest weight possible for any land animal. If they were any heavier their legs (right) would have been so large they wouldn't have been able to move.

Elephant Bird

The largest prehistoric bird was the flightless 'elephant bird' (right) which lived in Australia between 15 million and 25,000 years ago. It is believed to have been about 3m tall and weighed around 500kg.

Early Bird

Archaeopteryx (right), the earliest primitive bird, probably couldn't fly very well at all. It had feathers but its bones were solid and heavy, unlike the birds of today.

No Fear

The first amphibians had just 1 other creature to fear when they were on land. They shared their terrestrial world with scorpions.

Egg-laying Mammal

The duck-billed platypus — the only mammal apart from the echidnas of Australia and New Guinea to lay eggs — is the most primitive living mammal on Earth. It has existed for 150 million years in Australia's streams and rivers.

Prehistoric Relic

The tuatara lizard, found in New Zealand, is the last survivor of a group of prehistoric reptiles. Its eggs take 15 months to hatch, and it then takes another 20 years to grow into an adult.

Sea Dwellers

Sea creatures called trilobites had large, round eyes with more than 1000 lenses.

The giant sea creature Elasmosaurus had 76 vertebrae in its backbone, the largest number of any animal ever known.

Sponges, which feed by drawing in water through pores on their body surface, have remained almost unchanged for 600 million years.

❖

A fish called the coelacanth was believed to have been extinct for 70 million years until it was rediscovered in the waters off the African coast in 1938.

First Flowers

The first plants grew on land about 400 million years ago, but it was another 250 million years before the first flowers appeared.

Flying Dragon

The prehistoric dragonfly *Meganeura* (left) had a wingspan of 72cm, making it the world's largest ever insect. It flew in the Palaeozoic skies around 300 million years ago.

Early Mammals

Woolly Giant

Mammoths (right) were large, hairy-coated, elephant-like creatures that lived between 2 million and 11,000 years ago. Mammoths found deep-frozen in Siberia still had blood in their bodies. The remains of over 1000 mammoths have been found at a prehistoric settlement in the former Czechoslovakia.

Half Mammal

Cynognathus was half mammal and half reptile. Its name means 'jaws of a dog'. It may have been covered in fur, but it laid eggs like a reptile.

Giant Deer

Until 50,000 years ago, giant deer with antlers 2.5m wide roamed the Earth.

Hoofless

Only about the size of a fox, Eohippus was the first horse. This little animal still had toes instead of hooves. It lived in forests.

Egg Hunters

The first mammals, small, shrew-like creatures, lived at the same time as the dinosaurs and probably feasted on their eggs.

Giant Rhinoceros

The largest land mammal that has ever been recorded was Baluchitherium (left), which lived about 35 million years ago. A kind of hornless rhinoceros, it was tall enough to look over the roof of a 2-storey house, and 6 people could have walked side by side underneath its belly.

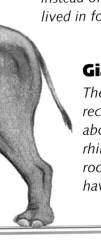

Natural Disasters

Unlucky For Some

A thunderstorm over Lapleau in France in 1968 killed all of the black sheep in a flock (left) but left the white ones unharmed.

Mountain Ash

In AD79 Mount Vesuvius exploded, covering the Italian city of Pompeii under 6m of volcanic ash and killing 20,000 people. Excavation of the city began in 1748, and now whole streets and buildings can be seen.

Black Death

The Black Death, or bubonic plague, struck in the middle of the 14th century, leaving a quarter of Europe's population dead.

Terror On Tambora

The greatest-known volcanic eruption, Tambora in Indonesia, claimed the lives of 90,000 people in April 1815.

Cloudy Skies

Clouds of sulphur from the Philippine volcano Mount Pinatuba affected the weather worldwide in 1991.

Wind And Water

◆ In April 1989, the world's worst tornado disaster left the town of Shaturia in Bangladesh devastated and 1300 people dead.

◆ The streets of Shiogama in Japan were littered with small boats after a massive earthquake in Chile in May 1960 sent giant tsunami waves across 16,000km of ocean in just 24 hours.

◆ Some 15 million trees were uprooted when hurricane-force winds hit Britain in October 1987.

◆ In 1931, an 83-tonne railway carriage with 117 passengers on board was picked up by a tornado and dropped into a ditch.

◆ When Hurricane Andrew hit Florida (right) in August 1992 it caused an estimated $22 million worth of damage, the highest of any natural disaster in US history.

◆ Up to 230,000 people died when the Banqiao and Shimantan dams burst in China in August 1975.

◆ In 1993, scientists reported the discovery of the greatest flood in history. The bursting of an ice-dam in Siberia had released a lake 120km long and 760m deep. Fortunately, this disaster occurred around 18,000 years ago.

◆ A cyclone and tidal wave killed 20,000 people in Bangladesh in 1963. Seven years later another 1 million were killed in a similar disaster.

◆ In 1972, more than 130 people were killed in a flash flood in Big Thompson Canyon, Colorado, USA. Nearly 25cm of rain had fallen in just a few hours.

Earthquakes

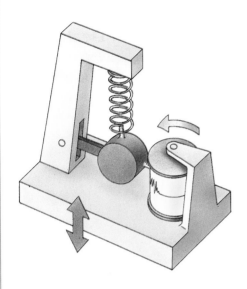

Seismic Measurer
The force and direction of earthquakes can be recorded on a seismograph (left). It has been estimated that there are 500,000 detectable seismic disturbances every year, though many are very small.

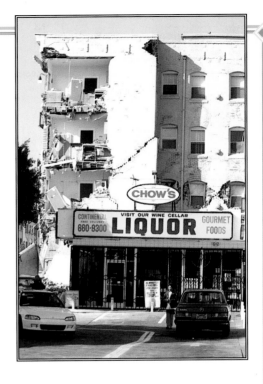

Total Destruction
An earthquake in July 1976 killed 750,000 people and flattened the Chinese city of Tangshan.

Strongest Tremor
The strongest earthquake ever recorded struck Chile on 22 May 1960.

London Shocker
Serious earthquakes are rare in England but a tremor in London in 1580 killed 2 people.

LA Flaw
The city of Los Angeles (above, as it appeared after the earthquake of January 1995) stands on the San Andreas fault, one of the most spectacular and active faults in the world.

Avalanche!
The world's worst known avalanche, on Huascarán mountain in Peru, killed 18,000 people in May 1970.

Drought In The Sahel
For the last 20 years there have been almost constant droughts in the Sahel region of Africa. The unreliable rain quickly drains away and people are unable to feed themselves or their livestock. Millions face starvation.

Modern Plague
The plague that ravaged 14th-century Europe still exists today. In 1994 pneumonic plague broke out in India.

Winter Of '77
In America, the winter of 1877 was so cold that there was frost in the town of Frostfree, Florida.

Flu Epidemic
The worldwide influenza epidemic that followed the 1st World War lasted from 1918 to 1919, and killed 21,640,000 people.

Crawling Clouds
In July 1875, enormous clouds of locusts (right) swooped down on Nebraska, USA, destroying vegetation across thousands of kilometres. The swarms, covering an estimated 514,000sq km, left 10,000 people destitute.

Odd Events And Disasters

Lighthouse

In December 1890, 3 men mysteriously vanished from a lighthouse on one of the Hebridean islands off Scotland (right). The men disappeared during fine weather when the sea was calm. The islanders searched everywhere, but they were never seen again. No answer has ever been found to the mystery of their disappearance.

Blue Moon

In 1950, raging forest fires in Canada sent up vast clouds of dust into the upper atmosphere, causing the moon to appear blue for several days.

Shrouded In Mystery

For many years, the Shroud of Turin, a linen cloth bearing the imprint of a man's face, wearing a crown of thorns, was believed by many to be the burial cloth of Jesus Christ.

Baby Boom

Mrs Barbara Zulu of South Africa set a new record when she gave birth to 6 sets of twins in only 7 years. Born between 1967 and 1973, her family finally comprised 3 sets of girls and 3 boy-girl sets.

Troubled Waters

In 1974, the *QE2* suffered inexplicable electrical and mechanical failure while sailing through the Bermuda Triangle. A nearby ship lost the *QE2* from its radar screen.

Balls Of Fire

Ball lightning appears as a fiery red, orange and yellow ball that floats above ground for several seconds before vanishing. It has been seen in houses and even in aeroplanes.

Hoof Of The Devil

In the winter of 1885, a track of cloven hoof prints extending for some 160km through snow across the countryside of Devon, England, were discovered. The tracks were traced over walls, across roofs and haystacks. The creature that made the tracks has never been identified. Some people believe them to have been the work of the devil.

Life And Death

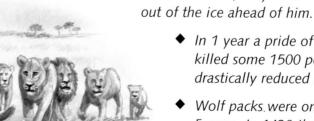

◆ A British ambulance driver, washing his vehicle in an Iranian river, nearly lost a leg when attacked by a shark (right) that had swum 140km upriver from the sea.

◆ One of Shackleton's Antarctic team of 1914–16 came close to death when he met a 3.5m leopard seal. It chased him across the ice and then dived into the water, only to break out of the ice ahead of him.

◆ In 1 year a pride of lions (left) in Kenya attacked and killed some 1500 people. The number of lions has been drastically reduced in recent years.

◆ Wolf packs were once common in wild places all over Europe. In 1420 the citizens of Paris, France, were horrified to find wolves roaming the capital's streets.

Two brothers died exactly 1 year apart riding the same moped down the same street and carrying the same passenger.

During the 2nd World War a rocket struck the British Museum and passed through a hole made by an earlier rocket. Both rockets luckily failed to explode.

The extinction of the dinosaurs 65 million years ago may be due to the crash of a meteorite near the Gulf of Mexico.

Mark Twain was born in 1835, the year Halley's comet appeared. He died in 1910, the year the comet reappeared.

Of the 8 Presidents of the USA who have died in office, 7 were elected at precisely 20-year intervals.

Abandoned Ship

The disappearance of the crew of the *Marie-Celeste*, an empty ship found floating undamaged off the coast of Portugal in 1872, remains one of the unsolved mysteries of the sea.

The Iceberg Cometh

Fourteen years before the sinking of the *Titanic* (right), a fictitious novel was written about a ship named *Titan*, which sinks on her maiden voyage. The fatal damage to *Titan* is also caused by hitting an iceberg. Incredibly, the *Titan* was supposed to be on the same route the *Titanic* followed on her first and last voyage in 1912.

Falling From The Sky

Hailstones

In 1888, hailstones killed more than 246 people in Moradabad in northern India.

Lightning

In the United States some 100 people are fatally struck by lightning every year. Many more are seriously injured.

The Iceman Cometh

In 1930 a German newspaper reported an extraordinary story: it claimed that 5 men encased in ice had dropped to Earth out of a thundercloud over the Rhön Mountains of central Germany.

Ghostly Profile

Twenty-five years after the death of Henry Liddell, dean of Christ Church Cathedral, Oxford, and father of Alice — the girl for whom Lewis Carroll wrote his famous *Alice in Wonderland* books — his profile appeared as a damp outline on the wall of the cathedral. The stain on the wall was still recognizable 3 years later.

Isle Of Skye

On a day in 1849, the Isle of Skye, lying off the west coast of Scotland, was hit by a massive single block of ice (right). It was measured and found to be 6m in circumference.

Showers From Heaven

Most meteorites fall harmlessly into the seas. Some have hit houses and cars, but no one has ever been killed by one. Every year falling meteorite particles add some 5 million tonnes to the Earth's mass.

Raining Frogs

One day in 1973, frogs fell from the sky in thousands on the French village of Brignoles.

History's Tyrants

Head Man

In 1387, Tartar warlord Tamerlane, who ruled land from China to Turkey, ordered reprisals for an attack. His army beheaded 70,000 people and piled up the heads in heaps.

Fond Farewell?

Henry VIII made his 2nd wife, Anne Boleyn, spend her last night before her execution in the room she had used on her coronation eve.

European Leaders

◆ Italian dictator Benito Mussolini (right) suffered a lifetime of expulsions: first from school for knifing fellow pupils, then from the Socialist party and finally from the Fascist party that had brought him to power.

◆ In 1937, German dictator and failed artist Adolf Hitler proposed that popular modern artists such as Otto Dix, Max Beckmann and George Grosz be dealt with under a programme for sterilizing the insane.

◆ For 36 years, General Francisco Franco ruled Spain without allowing any opposition or criticism.

Tyrants The World Over

Uncle Joe

In the 1930s, Russian dictator Joseph Stalin launched the Great Terror, a series of purges and executions that claimed the lives of 10 million people.

Brute Force

During China's Cultural Revolution of 1966–1977, Mao Zedong allowed his Red Army to torture 1000s of intellectuals and artists, and kill some 400,000 Chinese.

Flashy Bokassa

In 1977, Jean Bedel Bokassa (left) crowned himself Emperor Bokassa I of the Central African Empire. The ceremony, which cost about $200 million, bankrupted the country's economy. He was eventually deposed and sentenced to life imprisonment for murder.

No More Mr Nice Guy...

Idi Amin of Uganda (below) expelled the country's entire Asian population for 'sabotaging' the economy.

Mass Arrests

Augusto Pinochet, Chile's dictator, arrested, killed and exiled 10s of 1000s of opponents to his 1973 military coup.

Mass Murders

During Cambodia's Khmer Rouge regime (1975–1979), led by Pol Pot, over 2 million people died through disease, starvation and the mass execution of all opponents.

Fatal Fantasies

Queen Ranavalona of Madagascar executed any of her subjects who appeared in her dreams.

Tough Cookie

Rasputin (below), favourite of Tsar Nicholas II of Russia's wife, Alexandra, proved hard to assassinate. He was fed poisoned cakes and wine, shot through the chest, clubbed over the head and thrown into the frozen Neva River. An autopsy revealed he died from drowning.

Head Of State

Russia's greatest tsar, Peter the Great, was a bloodthirsty and vengeful man. He had his wife's lover executed and his head put into a jar of alcohol. He then forced his mourning wife to keep the preserved head in her bedroom.

Vlad the Impaler

Vlad ('Dracula') IV of Wallachia allied with Hungary in 1461 to conquer Turkish Bulgaria. Crossing the Danube, he killed 25,000 people by impaling them on stakes.

Buried Boffins

Rulers of China's Ch'in Dynasty (221–207BC) embarked on a programme to discourage learning and the teachings of the philosopher Confucius. They had numerous scholars and teachers buried alive.

Grisly Gardener

Abbad el Motaddid of Seville, Moorish king of Spain, used enemies' skulls as flowerpots.

Fiery Faith

The religious fanatic Tomas de Torquemada ruled the Spanish Inquisition. As Grand Inquisitor, he had 2000 people burned alive at the stake.

Rotten Relatives

The Duke of Bisceglie, 19-year-old husband of Lucrezia Borgia, was wounded in an assassination attempt. While recovering, he was strangled by a servant of infamous Cesare Borgia, Lucrezia's brother.

Terrible Ivan

Ivan the Terrible of Russia was so pleased with the newly built church of St Basil in Moscow that in 1555 he blinded the two architects, Postnik and Barma, so that they would never be able to outdo this masterpiece.

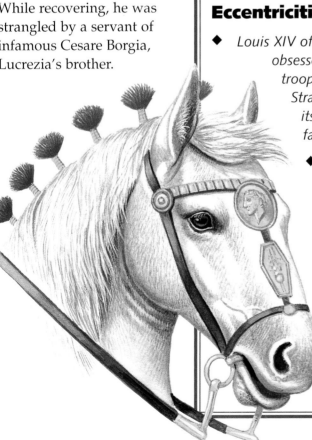

Eccentricities

◆ Louis XIV of France, the Sun King, was obsessed with fashion. When his troops occupied the city of Strasbourg in 1681, he ordered its citizens to adopt French fashions (right) within 4 months.

◆ China's first emperor, Shih Huang Ti, had his treasure-filled tomb booby-trapped with crossbows to keep out robbers.

◆ In the 16th century, François I of France made wearing whiskers punishable by death.

◆ Roman Emperor Caligula, infamous for murdering his relatives, also made his horse a consul (left).

◆ In Ancient Sparta, 7-year-old boys were trained as soldiers. They were forbidden to wear clothes until the age of 12.

Castle Secrets

Defence

Keep Out!

The guard towers of many castle ruins still standing have channels running down each side of the wall. This is where the raised metal portcullis, shown right (1), slid down to keep out unwanted intruders. Anyone trying to slip underneath risked being spiked by the sharp prongs along its base.

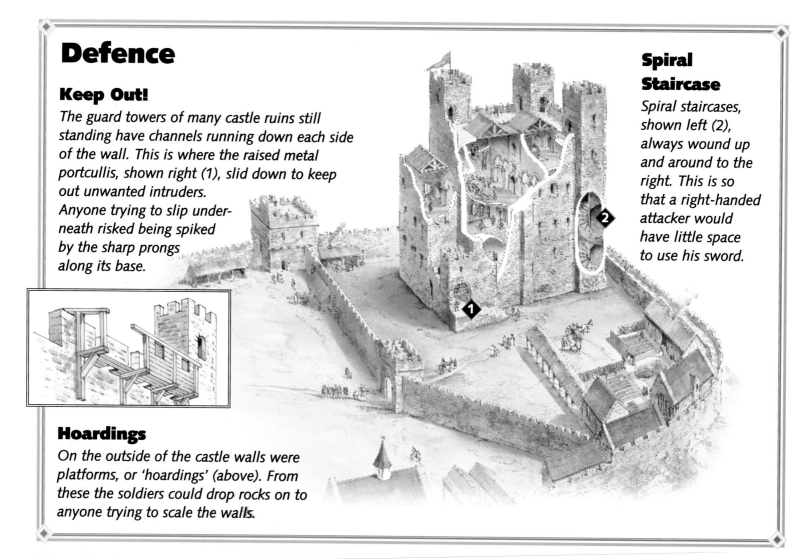

Spiral Staircase

Spiral staircases, shown left (2), always wound up and around to the right. This is so that a right-handed attacker would have little space to use his sword.

Hoardings

On the outside of the castle walls were platforms, or 'hoardings' (above). From these the soldiers could drop rocks on to anyone trying to scale the walls.

First Castle

The earliest castle was built at Gomdan in the Yemen. Originally built with 20 storeys, it dates from before the 1st century AD.

Largest Castle

The largest castle in the world is Hradcany Castle in Prague, Czech Republic. It covers an area of 7.28ha.

Windsor Castle

The world's largest inhabited castle is Windsor Castle in Berkshire, England.

Royal Flush

Bodiam Castle in Sussex, England, had some 30 toilets, all of which emptied into the moat.

Land Of Castles

Castile in central Spain is so named because so many castles were built there by Moors and Christians during the Middle Ages.

Fairytale Castle

The famous 'fairytale' castle, Schloss Neuschwanstein, in Germany, was actually built in the 19th century for Ludwig II, the mad King of Bavaria.

The Iron Mask

The famous 'Man in the Iron Mask' (left) died in Paris's Bastille Castle in 1703 and was buried in great secrecy. Historians now think he may have been the half-brother of King Louis XIV.

Attack

◆ *Siege weapons like the trebuchet (right) could be dismantled and the various parts brought to the battleground on carts pulled by oxen.*

◆ *Skilled longbowmen of the 1300s and 1400s could fire up to 12 arrows a minute and could hit a target 90m away. The bow could be up to 1.8m long.*

◆ *Cannons for battering down the walls of castles were first introduced in the early 1300s, but they were so poorly made that they often exploded in the gunners' faces.*

◆ *During a siege, attackers sometimes hurled dead animals and severed heads over the castle walls in an attempt to spread disease amongst the defenders.*

◆ *Battering rams (above right), used to smash down the castle gate, were covered in a frame of wet animal skins. These frames were called 'sows' or 'cats'.*

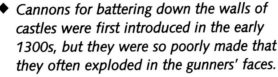

Building A Castle

The biggest medieval castles needed as many as 3000 men to build them, and could take as long as 20 years to complete.

Castle Collectors

In the Middle Ages, wealthy lords and nobles often owned more than 1 castle. England's King John owned over 100!

Californian Castle

In 1927, the American newspaper magnate William Randolph Hearst built himself a fairytale castle at San Simeon in California, USA, which he filled with treasures from around the world. At the time, it was the most costly home ever built.

Useful Castle

Since it was built in 1078, the Tower of London has housed a zoo, an observatory, a prison, a royal palace and a mint, as well as now being the home of the British Crown Jewels.

Japanese Castle

Although castle building declined in Europe following the development of cannons, in Japan it continued to flourish. The spectacular Himeji Castle (above) was still being added to up until about 1600.

Last Rites

Tombs

Body On View
Lenin died in 1924, but his preserved body is still on display inside a transparent coffin in a tomb in Moscow.

Silent Army
When Chinese Emperor Shih Huang Ti died in 210BC, 7500 terracotta archers, soldiers, chariots and horses (right) were buried with him in his tomb.

Petra
Some 2000 years ago in Petra, South Jordan, dramatic tombs were carved into the pink and purple cliff faces by the Nabataean Arabs.

Agamemnon
Agamemnon, the legendary king who led the combined Greek forces against Troy, sacrificed his daughter Iphigenia to the goddess Artemis and was murdered in the bath by his wife.

Grand Exit
The word mausoleum, meaning a grand tomb, derives from King Mausolus of Caria, whose tomb was very grand indeed.

Tutankhamun
The tomb of Egyptian boy-king Tutankhamun, discovered in 1922, contained nearly 2000 treasures, many of them all or part gold (left).

Hagia Sophia
Emperor Justinian I's church of Hagia Sophia in Constantinople (now Istanbul, Turkey) became his tomb when he died in AD565.

Dead Servile
Sixty of Queen Shub-Ad of Ur's servants were killed and buried with her, ready to serve her in the afterlife.

Day Of The Dead
In Mexico, the Day of the Dead festival is held every year on 2 November. People visit the graves of their relatives and give each other skull-shaped sweets.

Tombs of Treacle
In Boston, USA, 21 people were killed in 1919 by a 2 million gallon tank of molasses that burst and engulfed 8 buildings.

Catacombs
The most elaborate underground tombs were those built by the early Christians. They buried their dead in a labyrinth of catacombs (left) in Ancient Rome and other places around the Mediterranean.

Stone Cold

It is so cold in Siberia that gravediggers have to pour paraffin on the ground and set light to it before they can thaw the subsoil enough to make digging possible.

Customs

❖

Until outlawed by the British in the 19th century, suttee, *the burning of a widow on her husband's funeral pyre, was a custom in India for centuries.*

❖

The Parsee religious community places their dead on platforms, called towers of silence, for them to be picked over by vultures.

❖

It was an ancient custom in England for people who had committed suicide to be buried in unconsecrated ground at crossroads, or on the north side of churchyards. A stake driven through their bodies was thought to stop their spirits rising up and haunting the neighbourhood.

❖

Jews are buried facing Jerusalem, while Muslims face Mecca.

❖

After cremation, Hindus like to scatter the ashes of the person on a river or the sea.

Burial Mounds

One of the largest Native American burial mounds is Grave Creek Mound, West Virginia, USA, at 20m high and 100m wide.

Sugar Daddy

In 323BC, Alexander the Great (left) was taken ill and died after a banquet in Babylon. His body was kept preserved in honey until he was buried in a gold coffin in Alexandria.

Dead And Buried

Poor Mozart

Only 1 mourner walked beside Mozart's coffin before it was placed in a pauper's grave.

Just Whistle

When film star Humphrey Bogart died, his wife Lauren Bacall placed a whistle in his coffin, inscribed: "If you need anything, just whistle." This line was from the first film they made together, The Big Sleep.

Heart In The Right Place

Thomas Hardy's ashes were buried at Westminster Abbey, London, but his heart was first removed and buried in the grave of his first wife.

Bootleg O'Banion

The greatest gangster funeral was that of a bootlegger called Dion O'Banion. Some 10,000 mourners attended and a $1000 wreath was paid for by Al Capone, who had ordered O'Banion's execution.

Be Prepared!

Sailors (below) used to wear gold earrings to pay for the cost of a proper burial.

Groggy

The body of Admiral Horatio Nelson (above) was preserved in a barrel of rum on its journey back to England after the Battle of Trafalgar. It is buried in St Paul's Cathedral, London.

Crime And Punishment

Ancient Punishments

Keep Mum!

A Medieval branks, or scold's bridle, was an iron cage fitted round the head of a nagging wife to keep her quiet. Some branks had spiked tongue plates.

Pilloried

Dishonest traders in Medieval times were put in a pillory (below), a contraption with holes for the victim's head and hands. Passers-by would throw dung at them.

Hanging Horse

The largest-existing Roman bronze sculpture, a statue of Emperor Marcus Aurelius, was used as a gibbet in AD965.

Stock Still

In Medieval times, thieves and drunkards were put in the stocks, a wooden bench with leg-irons.

For The Chop

The guillotine, used to chop off heads during the French Revolution, was the official means of execution in France until 1981.

Out For A Duck

A Medieval ducking stool was a chair on the end of a pole. Scolding women were fastened to it and plunged into a river, a pond, or even a cesspit.

'Lucky' Luciano

The powerful US Mafia boss was nicknamed 'Lucky' because he escaped death so often.

Bulky Booty

The largest object ever stolen by a single person was a ship (below), cut from its Canadian moorings in 1966.

Highway Robbery

Mary Frith, who was born in London in 1584, trained as a seamstress. Unable to endure a quiet life, she became a pickpocket. Taking the name of Moll Cutpurse, she dressed as a man (below) and with her gang of thieves made a fortune by robbing unsuspecting travellers on wild and deserted roads.

Fatal Error

The abolition of the death penalty in Britain was triggered by the case of John Evans. Hanged in 1950 for the supposed murder of his baby daughter, Evans was later proved innocent. He was granted a free pardon 16 years after his death on the gallows.

Modern Criminals

❖

In the 1990 Guinness trial in London, Gerald Ronson received a record-breaking £5 million fine.

❖

Lee Harvey Oswald, US President Kennedy's assassin in 1963, was himself assassinated before he could be brought to trial.

❖

During the Great Train Robbery of 1963, a record-breaking £2,631,784 was stolen from a mail train between Glasgow and London.

Transportation

Transporting criminals and ordinary citizens to the colonies (below) was a lucrative trade for London businessmen during the 18th century.

Witch Hunt

At the end of the 17th century, 150 alleged witches were condemned in the town of Salem, Massachusetts, USA.

Double Standard

US Sheriff Henry Plummer led a gang of bandits at night.

Radio Copped

Recognized as he made his escape aboard ship, Dr Crippen was the first murderer to be caught by the use of radio-telegraphy.

Knife Man

Jack the Ripper terrorized the East End of London in 1888, when he cut the throats of 5 women. Guesses at his identity include a royal duke, a doctor and a barrister.

Legendary Outlaws

Armour-plated

Ned Kelly, the famous 19th-century Australian bank robber, wore home-made armour. On the run for 2 years, his capture and that of his gang cost £115,000.

Kids' Stuff

Henry McCarty, also called William Bonney (right), was best known as Billy the Kid. A killer from the age of 12, he was notorious throughout the Wild West for cattle rustling, hold-ups and robberies. He was finally caught by Sheriff Pat Garrett in 1881 and accused of killing 21 men — 1 for each year of his short life.

Taxing

Al Capone (left), the vicious Chicago gangster, was eventually imprisoned for tax evasion rather than murder.

Disloyal

After 15 years of robbing banks, Jesse James was killed by his own cousin. Bob Ford, a member of Jesse's gang, killed the legendary outlaw for a $10,000 reward.

Axe Woman

In 1892, US citizen Lizzie Borden was accused of killing her parents with an axe. Despite the evidence against her, she was acquitted during a sensational trial.

Body-snatchers

Eighteenth-century criminals William Burke and William Hare suffocated unsuspecting travellers in a Scottish lodging house. The corpses, which were sold for anatomical dissection, fetched up to £14 each. It is thought that at least 16 people were disposed of in this way.

Travellers' Tales

Biking

Tricycles are not allowed to be ridden at over 16kph in Vancouver, Canada.

East Meets West

The rickshaw (left) a vehicle pulled along by 1 or 2 people, is often associated with Japan and the Far East. Who would have thought that it was invented in 1888 by an American Baptist minister?

Cold Comfort

In 1939, an ancient city made up of 800 houses was discovered in Alaska, USA, 209km inside the Arctic Circle.

Tall Tales

When Marco Polo returned from the East, people disbelieved his accounts of Chinese inventions, such as gunpowder.

Pacific Tales

Trieste

Follow The Leaders

Vasco de Balboa's expedition to the Pacific in 1513 was led by bloodhounds.

Remarkable Family

Swiss twins Auguste and Jean Piccard shared a spirit of adventure. In 1931 Auguste made a balloon ascent of 16km. Jean, a professor of engineering, designed a balloon in which he made a 17.5km ascent 3 years later. Turning his attention to the depths, in 1948 Auguste explored the ocean off West Africa in a bathyscaphe of his own design. Auguste's son Jacques then broke all records with the crew of the US bathyscaphe Trieste (right), which dived 11km beneath the surface of the Pacific.

Keep Quiet

A law on the Pacific island of Pitcairn prohibits the shouting of 'Sail ho' — a traditional cry on sighting an approaching ship — when there is no ship to be seen.

Limey Sailor

British sailors got the nickname 'limey' after they were issued with lime juice to combat the disease scurvy in 1795.

Bottled Up

A bottle with a message in it, dropped into the Pacific in 1941, was picked up on a remote island 2000km away 53 days later. Unfortunately, the islander who found it could not read any of the 8 languages in which the message was written.

Whatever Next?

◆ The galaxy M74 (right) is 80,000 light years across. Yet there are others in the universe more than 80 times bigger than the M74 galaxy.

◆ A type of giant clam found on the coast of Malaysia is large enough to devour a person.

◆ Magellan's crew were so hungry while crossing the Pacific that they ate the ship's rats and the leather straps off the masts.

◆ St John's Lane in Rome is only 48cm wide.

◆ The Great Pyramid of Cheops in Egypt contains enough stone to build a wall 3m high all around France.

◆ In 1964, an aircraft flying over Chicago, USA, was struck by lightning 5 times in 20 minutes without causing major damage.

◆ While searching for fellow explorer David Livingstone in central Africa, Henry Moreton Stanley reported seeing chimpanzees carrying burning torches marching at night (left).

Snow House

Many Europeans believe that all Eskimos live in igloos built from carefully cut blocks of frozen snow. A census in 1920, however, revealed that fewer than 1 Eskimo in 46 had ever seen an igloo.

Back To Front

The Panama Canal is the only place where you can see the sun rise over the Pacific and set over the Atlantic.

Mummy's Curse

Ten people connected with the opening of Tutankhamun's tomb in Egypt in 1922 died of unnatural causes.

Chess Men

More people play chess in the former Soviet Union than anywhere else.

Big Mistake

Christopher Columbus discovered America for Spain in 1492 — but he died still believing the land he had found was really Asia.

Desert Drawings

In the Nazca Desert of Peru, huge drawings have been found etched on the ground. Although thought to have been made by Indians 1000 years ago, they can only be seen properly from the air. This has prompted some people to suggest that they are connected to visitors from outer space.

Bristol Fashion

Explorers crossing Alaska, USA, reported seeing a strange mirage. Usually these take the form of a distorted image or a sheet of water, but what the explorers saw was the English city of Bristol on the Alaskan skyline! The city is in fact approximately 10,500km away.

Final Cut

Samurai warriors (right) were bound by a strict code of honour. If captured or defeated in battle they were obliged to kill themselves in a very painful manner. Their suicide took the form of a ritual disembowelling known as 'Hari Kiri'.

Madonna's Tears

In 1982 a Spanish statue of the Virgin was said to weep tears of blood.

Lucky Escapes

Up A Mountain

✤

Chris Bonington and Doug Scott fell badly on Ogre Mountain in the Karakorums, Pakistan. Bonington broke his ribs and Scott broke both legs. But they managed to descend on hands and knees; it took 6 days.

✤

Sixteen survivors from a plane crash in the Andes managed to live by eating the flesh of their dead companions.

No Justice

When Mount Pelée on Martinique (below) erupted in 1902, the only survivor in St Pierre was a prisoner in the town jail.

Rough Times

After the mutiny on the *Bounty* in 1879, Captain William Bligh and 18 men were cast adrift in a small boat (above). Land was sighted 47 days and 9370km later, after a journey with few provisions and no maps.

Dying Of Thirst

In 1840, Englishman Edward Eyre set out from Adelaide to find a route to Albany in southwestern Australia. His life was saved by his Aborigine companion, who dug down nearly 3m to find him water.

Snow-bound

In 1978, a shepherd found a ewe alive after it had been buried in deep snow for 50 days.

Baby In Trouble

Baby Juana Arias was 1 day old when she was buried alive for 8 days under the rubble of the Juarez Hospital, following an earthquake in Mexico City in 1985.

No Noose

Playwright Ben Jonson was jailed for murder in 1598. He escaped the gallows by claiming his right as a clergyman not to be hanged. Later he became England's first poet laureate.

Animal Mayhem

◆ *In 1596, Dutch explorer Willem Barents went in search of a Northeast Passage from Europe to Asia. Only after narrowly escaping the savage attack of a polar bear (right), on land he named Bear Island, was he able to continue the expedition.*

◆ *Famous explorer David Livingstone nearly lost his life when his boat was overturned in mid-stream by a hippopotamus.*

◆ *Sailor James Bartley was rescued from the belly of a whale 1 day after falling overboard near the Falkland Islands.*

◆ *In 1567, Spaniard Álvaro de Mendaña set sail from Peru. A day later his ship hit a sleeping whale, but survived! It later lost a mast in a hurricane, but Mendaña carried on, and finally discovered the Solomon Islands.*

Mid-air Escapes

Strip Down

Balloonists (below), making the first successful crossing of the English Channel, averted disaster by throwing their clothes overboard to make the balloon lighter.

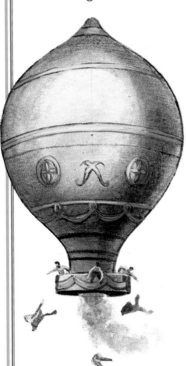

Mission Impossible

In April 1970, quick-thinking American astronauts on Apollo 13 (left) managed to return to Earth safely, despite the explosion of an oxygen tank in the service module en route to the Moon.

Free Fall

A 2nd World War crewman fell from a burning British bomber without a parachute and landed in undergrowth, surviving a free fall of 5500m.

High Impact

US parachutist Eddie Turner saved his unconscious colleague in 1988 by pulling the ripcord of his parachute 10 seconds before he hit the ground.

Twice Alive

In 1972, an air hostess survived a fall of over 10,000m after a mid-air explosion.

High Science

In 1956, 2 US scientists survived, without pressure suits or goggles, an accidental open-air ascent by airship to 12,840m.

Desperate Measures

In 1969, a Cuban stowaway hid in the wing cavity of an airliner. He survived a 9000km flight at an altitude of over 10,000m, in temperatures of -22°C.

Slipping The Noose

In 1650, Anne Green was hanged for murder. When her body was cut down from the gallows, however, she was found to be alive. She is said to have recovered and lived to a great age.

Real Life

The story of Robinson Crusoe was inspired by the life of Alexander Selkirk (right), a Scottish sailor who was rescued from a Pacific island where he had been stranded for over 4 years.

Chief Witness

Pliny the Younger, the Ancient Roman scholar, saw Pompeii engulfed by lava, but survived unharmed. In a letter to Tacitus he wrote the first known eyewitness account of a volcanic eruption.

Desperate Measures

Desert travellers desperate for water have been known to kill camels and give the water in their stomachs to their horses.

Snowed Under

In 1755, 3 Italian women survived for 37 days in a stable that had been buried by an avalanche.

Why Diet?

A 125kg Icelander, who had a 14mm layer of fat all over his body, survived 6 hours in icy water and 3 hours walking across a frozen lava field in just his jeans and a shirt.

Monster Sightings

Human Monsters

Elephant Man
John Merrick, the 'Elephant Man' (left), suffered a terrible disorder causing physical deformities. His head grew to 1m in circumference. He only lived to be 27 years old.

You Great Ape!
In 1967, a huge, hairy, ape-like creature was caught on film in Bluff Creek, Utah, USA.

Howlin' Wolf
In the past, people suspected of being werewolves (able to turn into wolf-creatures at night) were tortured and burned to death.

Castle Creep
Glamis Castle in Scotland was said to be the home of a monster (above) that lived there for 200 years, up until the 1920s.

Old Bones
Fossilized bones of prehistoric animals were, in past centuries, believed to be the bones of giants.

Mythical Carving
The giant chalk man hewn into the hillside at Cerne Abbas, England, is thought to represent Hercules.

Barking Mad...
In 1975, 5 men in present-day Croatia stood trial after being found trying to burn to death an alleged witch. They argued that the woman had taken the form of a large dog and attacked them.

...Dog's Dinner
One Sunday morning in August 1577, 2 church services in Suffolk, England, were thrown into panic by the appearance of a monstrous black dog (below), which killed 2 people in Bungay church and 3 in the village of Blythburgh, 11km away.

Everest Mystery
In 1951, Mount Everest mountaineers Eric Shipton and Michael Ward photographed tracks in the snow of an unidentified creature with footprints 33cm x 20cm.

Abominable Snowman
The yeti, or abominable snowman, is thought to inhabit the Himalayas near the snowline. Explorers there have found huge footprints in the snow. Some have reported sightings of tall creatures with pointed heads and huge hands.

Family Friend
In 1940, a family in Ruby Creek, California, USA, reported an incident in which they were approached by a hairy creature 2.44m tall. It left footprints 40cm long.

The Monster In Loch Ness

◆ *St Columba was famed for banishing the monster from Loch Ness (left). Subsequent 'sightings' suggest that he was not altogether successful.*

◆ *The most famous photograph of the Loch Ness monster was taken by a London surgeon in 1934. The date? 1 April.*

◆ *The naturalist Sir Peter Scott and an American researcher gave Nessie the scientific name Nessiteras rhombopteryx, an anagram of the words 'monster hoax by Sir Peter S'.*

◆ *A trail of 'monster' footprints was discovered in the soft ground around the edge of Loch Ness. But the experts were not fooled. The footprints had been made using a hippopotamus-foot umbrella stand.*

Kidnapped By Bigfoot

In 1924, Canadian lumberman Albert Ostman claimed to have been kidnapped by a strange creature and carried 40km to its lair. Ostman managed to escape after 6 days in captivity.

The Living Dead

Powerful natural drugs can cause people to seem dead. The victims are called zombies.

Dragon Slayer

The dragon killed by St George was said to represent the Devil in the Middle Ages.

Sea Monsters

What A Sucker!

The largest squid ever found had an eye 0.5m across and tentacles with suckers the size of saucers.

Big Smoothie

In Chesapeake Bay in the USA there have been sightings of a dark, smooth-skinned sea serpent up to 10m long.

Mermaid?

Sailors who claim they saw mermaids probably confused these mythical creatures with dugongs (above right). Dugongs are shy, slow-moving mammals found in warm waters.

Snake Head

In 1848, a sea creature 18m long, with snake-like head, a long neck and a flowing mane like seaweed (below) was spotted by sailors in the South Atlantic.

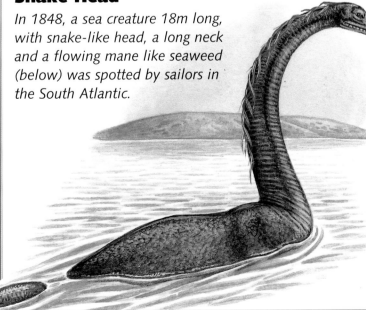

Giant Clam

The largest giant clam was found at Ishigaki Island, Japan in 1956. It weighed an incredible 333kg!

Huge Hug

The largest octopus ever caught was a monster measuring 7m from one tentacle-tip to another.

Collective Killer

The Portuguese man-of-war, with tentacles reaching up to 18m in length, is not one single animal but up to 1000 individuals all working together. They form a type of jellyfish killing machine with a poison nearly as strong as that of a cobra's.

They Were First

Into Space

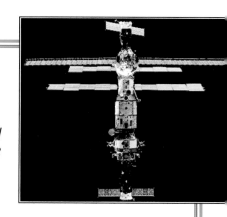

First Ever

The 1st man in space was Colonel Yuri Gagarin (left). He took off in Vostok 1 from the Baikonur cosmodrome in Kazakhstan, then part of the USSR. His record-breaking flight, which took place on 12 April 1961, ended 108 minutes later at Smelovka.

Space Sick

The 1st astronauts to travel in the Skylab craft in 1973 carried travel sickness pills.

Renewing Links

In 1995, Norman Thagard boarded the Russian space station Mir (above right), becoming the 1st American to enter an orbiting Russian craft in 20 years.

Germ-free

The first astronauts spent a fortnight in quarantine.

Transatlantic

In 1927, Charles Lindbergh was 1st to fly solo across the Atlantic. With an extra fuel tank blocking the windscreen, he had to use a periscope throughout the 33.5 hour flight to see where he was going.

Cavalry Creamery

Troops of Genghis Khan (1162-1227) were among the first to use powdered milk. They dried mare's milk in the sun to use on long horseback journeys.

Westward Ho!

In 1492, Columbus' crew (right) after only 2 weeks were afraid they would never return home. So Columbus kept 2 ship's log-books. A secret one recorded the real distances travelled, while the one on view had shorter, invented distances so the crew would think they were still quite close to home.

Solo Polar Traveller

The Japanese explorer Naomi Uemura was the first person to travel alone to the North Pole. Setting off from Ellesmere Island, he covered more than 720km by dog sled, arriving at the Pole on 1 May 1978.

High Flyer

In 1937, Amelia Earhart became the first woman to fly around the world. The cockpit of her plane was just 1.5sq m.

Moving Ships

In 1851, sailors found 2 ships from John Franklin's Northwest Passage expedition of 1845–1847 locked in ice, 3200km away from their former anchorage.

On Top Of The World

❖

In 1873, Isabella Bird Bishop was the 1st European woman to reach the top of Mauna Loa, the Hawaiian volcano.

❖

In 1953, Sir Edmund Hillary and Sherpa Tenzing were the 1st people to reach the summit of Mount Everest.

The 1524m north face of the Eiger, a notoriously difficult climb, was not conquered until 1938.

The first official mountaineering expedition took place on the remote Scottish island of St Kilda in 1698.

❖

Martin Stone was the 1st person to climb all 8 Scottish peaks over 1219m high. It took him 21 hours 39 minutes.

On 10 May 1993, a total of 40 climbers in 9 separate expeditions all reached the summit of Mount Everest.

In 1970 Anapurna III was the 1st of the world's high mountains to be climbed by an all-women team.

Italian artist Leonardo da Vinci was one of the earliest mountain climbers. In the mid 16th century he climbed the southern slopes of the Apennines.

Travel Ace

Sir Richard Burton, 19th-century explorer and orientalist (left), was a man of many talents. His remarkable translation of *The Arabian Nights* is still popular today. He became famous when he entered Mecca disguised as a Muslim pilgrim in 1853. Five years later he and Sir John Hanning Speke became the 1st Westerners to discover and then explore Lake Tanganyika in Africa.

On The High Seas

Travelling Blind

In 1662 Abel Tasman sailed right around Australia without ever sighting it.

Territorial

Captain James Cook (right) claimed more territory for Britain than any other explorer. Here he is seen taking possession of New South Wales, Australia.

Kayak Travel

In 1928, Franz Romer became the 1st man to cross the Atlantic Ocean in a kayak. The journey took him 58 days.

First Time Round

The Phoenicians sailed round the Cape of Good Hope 2000 years before Bartholomew Diaz's 1486 expedition.

Around The World

With 5 ships and a crew of 270 men, Ferdinand Magellan, the Portuguese navigator, led the 1st expedition to sail round (circumnavigate) the globe in 1519–1521.

It's A 'Green Land'

The island of Greenland was discovered by Norseman Erik the Red in AD982. He sailed there from Iceland. Most of the island lies under a permanent ice cap, but Erik decided to call it 'Greenland' so as to encourage potential settlers. His ploy worked — a Norse colony was founded there in AD986 and lasted for 500 years.

High Climber

In 1908, Annie Peck (below) achieved 2 very different records. When she scaled the 6768m peak of Mount Huáscaran in Peru she became the first woman to climb to such a high altitude. She was also the 1st climber to wear an 'anorak', or Eskimo suit, which she borrowed from a museum.

Wild Places

Explorers

Ross, Ross, Ross

James Clarke Ross, Arctic and Antarctic explorer, had the Ross Ice Shelf, Ross Sea and Ross Island all named after him.

Near Miss

The 1907 polar expedition of Ernest Shackleton (left) got to within 156km of the South Pole, before turning back.

Footsore

During his explorations David Livingstone travelled more than 48,000km across central Africa, mostly on foot or by canoe.

Parisian Pilgrim

In 1924, Parisian Alexandra David-Néel was the 1st Western woman to reach the Tibetan capital, Lhasa. She was disguised as a poor Tibetan pilgrim.

Intrepid Woman

Freya Stark (1893–1993) spent years travelling in remote areas of the Middle East, usually alone except for local guides.

Ancient Cave Man

In 1906, the Hungarian-born, British archeologist Aurel Stein (above) discovered the Cave of 1000 Buddhas near Dunhuang in China. The cave had been walled up since the 11th century and contained priceless manuscripts and paintings dating from the 5th to the 10th centuries.

Empty Country

Greenland is almost 10 times the size of Britain yet has barely 1/1000th of Britain's population of nearly 60 million.

Cool Deal

The snowy wastes of Alaska were bought by the USA from Russia in 1867 for $7,700,000.

Mighty Rivers

Seventeen of the rivers flowing into the Amazon are themselves over 1600km long.

Desert Drought

Until 1973, no rain had fallen on some parts of the Atacama Desert in northern Chile for more than 400 years.

Pacific Ocean

Atlantic Ocean

Largest Rain Forest

The world's largest rain forest, the Amazon Rain Forest, covers an area of 6.5 million sq km and has a richer plant and animal life than anywhere in the world. Unfortunately, much of it is now being cut down for farmland.

Animals Of Wild Places

- ◆ High in the Pamir Mountains of Central Asia lives a breed of wild sheep with curled horns 1.5m long. They are called Marco Polo sheep after the 13th-century Venetian traveller.

- ◆ Przewalski's horse, the last wild species living today, was discovered on the remote Asian steppes in the 19th century by Nicolai Przewalski.

- ◆ In Africa, lions killed and ate 28 workers, delaying the building of the railway bridge between Mombasa and Lake Victoria at the end of the 19th century.

- ◆ Male emus (right) in the Australian outback bring up the family, not eating or drinking until the eggs have hatched.

Biggest Desert

The Sahara Desert in Africa, at 9 million sq km, is as large as the continent of Europe.

Ocean Of Islands

There are some 25,000 islands in the Pacific, but only a few thousand of them are inhabited.

Low Snow

Less snow falls in the Arctic lowlands each year than in the southern state of Virginia, USA.

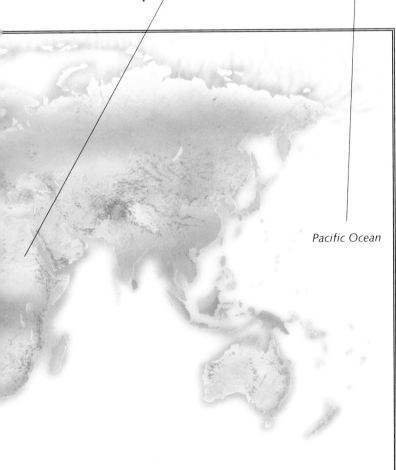

Pacific Ocean

Polar Regions

❖

The Antarctic icecap is reckoned to be over 2400m thick.

❖

The lowest temperature ever recorded on Earth was the -89°C measured at Vostock in Antarctica on 21 July 1983.

❖

The largest iceberg recorded is bigger than Belgium. It was an Antarctic tabular iceberg of over 31,000sq km sighted in 1956.

❖

During a severe blizzard in the polar regions visibility can be reduced to 1m.

❖

During the polar summer, when the Poles are facing towards the sun, it is light all day. During the polar winter, however, the sun never rises.

❖

The Inuit (Eskimos) crossed what was then a land bridge between Asia and North America around 6000 years ago.

Over The Top

The 1st journey from Europe to North America over the North Pole was made by airship in 1926. On board was Roald Amundsen (left), leader of the 1st expedition to reach the South Pole. He was also the 1st person to sail through the infamous Northwest Passage, a sea route from the Atlantic to the Pacific, north of Canada.

Strange Beliefs

Curious Cures

- *The Persians, believing that human tears could cure many afflictions, used to bottle them for future use.*

- *It was once thought that advice on treating whooping cough only worked if given by someone riding a piebald horse.*

- *The Irish cure for mumps used to involve leading the patient 3 times around a pigsty.*

- *In Ancient Rome fresh blood shed by a gladiator (left) was believed to cure people suffering from epilepsy.*

- *In Ancient Carthage, it was believed that one way to cure indigestion was to rub a cow's tail on your tummy (above right).*

- *In the 16th century, being breathed on by a billy goat was believed to give protection from the plague.*

Peacock Problem

Some actors believe that peacock feathers, or even mentioning peacocks, brings bad luck.

Flee Fleas!

In 1670, the authorities in the German state of Munster formally banished a plague of fleas, prohibiting them from returning for 10 years. The fleas, brought by rats, were carriers of the dreaded bubonic plague. It is not known how successful these unusual precautions were.

All Greek

Pythagoras, Greek philosopher of the 6th century BC, founded a club where members were forbidden to eat beans or to poke fires with iron implements. The beliefs behind these rules are unknown.

Dirty Beasts

In the 4th century BC, the Greek philosopher Aristotle believed that animals were created from mud and rotting flesh.

Bed-wetting

In the 19th century, British Prime Minister Benjamin Disraeli stood his bed legs in salted water, believing that this would ward off evil spirits.

Dangerous Moonlight

It is said that many Cuban people wear hats when they go out at night. There is a traditional Cuban belief that may explain this habit. It was said that moonlight exerted an evil influence if it shone directly on to a person's head.

Divided Womb

The ancient Greeks believed the womb had 1 compartment for girls and another for boys.

Dark Smile

Women in medieval Japan often painted their teeth black. Black teeth were prized at that time and considered to be signs of great beauty.

Egg-straordinary

The ancient Egyptians believed that the world was created when it hatched from the egg of the ibis (left), a wading bird with a long, curved bill. It is scarcely surprising that the ibis was considered by the ancient Egyptians to be a sacred bird.

Sticky End

Doctors in the 19th century believed that eating chewing gum caused the intestines to stick together.

Coffee Time

Food fads are nothing new. King Gustav III, the 18th-century ruler of Sweden, was convinced that coffee was lethally poisonous. So strong was his belief that he ordered a criminal to drink himself to death with coffee. The execution was not very successful. It lasted until the condemned man died of old age at 83.

Standing Still

In ancient times it was believed that kings and queens should be buried in an upright position, instead of lying down like their subjects.

Magnetic Prose

The famous novelist Charles Dickens believed that he had to face north when he wrote.

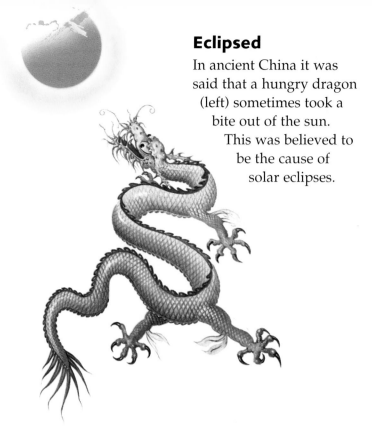

Eclipsed

In ancient China it was said that a hungry dragon (left) sometimes took a bite out of the sun. This was believed to be the cause of solar eclipses.

Love And Marriage

Ring Finger

In ancient times, before much was known about anatomy, people believed that the 3rd finger of the left hand (above) was linked directly to the heart. This is why wedding rings are worn on that finger in many cultures around the world.

What's In A Name?

In England people used to place great faith in names. For example, if a woman married a man with the same surname as her own, it was thought that she would automatically be endowed with special healing powers.

False Step

In some parts of France people still hold ancient beliefs about marriage. They think that a bachelor who steps on a cat's tail will not find a wife for at least a year.

Wedding Belles

On the eve of St Agnes, 21 January, girls would go to bed without supper. They believed that if they turned their eyes to heaven without looking to left or right, they would see a vision of their future husbands.

Sweet Dreams

In Sweden it was once believed that young women could see their future husbands in a dream once a year, on Midsummer night. The dream only occurred if a girl put 7 different wild flowers (right and above) under her pillow that night.

Astonishing Feats

Light Fantastic

The French painter Anne-Louis Girodet liked to work late into the night. In order to see he would light up to 40 candles on his hat brim (left). He based his fee on the number of candles burned while painting the picture.

Lung Power

Divers breathing pure oxygen for 30 minutes before descent have held their breath under water for 13 minutes.

Bundles Of Joy

Between 1725 and 1765, the wife of Russian peasant Feodor Vassilyev gave birth to 69 children. Only 2 died in infancy.

Punishing Performance

Indian swami Maujgiri Maharaj stood continuously for more than 17 years when performing penance. Even when asleep, he was held upright by a board.

Planning Ahead

The prophecies of 16th-century French astrologer Nostradamus have been interpreted as including submarines, war in the air, radio communication, Napoleon and Hitler.

Take A Walk

In 1809, Englishman Captain Barclay walked 1609km (1000 miles) in 1000 hours, an average of 23.8 hours per day for 42 days. He lost 14kg in weight.

Unusual Physical Feats

Aristocratic Ears

Eighteenth-century Empress Marie Louise, daughter of Francis I of Austria and 2nd wife of Napoleon, had an unusual ability to move her ears at will and even to turn them inside out.

No Fear!

A French actor called Pierre Mes (right) could make his hair stand on end whenever he chose.

Face Value

English billiard player Henry Lewis (below), could play with his nose instead of a cue.

Gentleman

Nineteenth-century boxer 'Gentleman' Jackson could sign his name with a 36kg ball on his arm.

Record-breaking Teeth

In 1992, Armenian strongman Robert Galstyan pulled 2 coupled railway wagons weighing 219 tonnes a distance of 7m — with his teeth! He did it using a steel cable attached to the 1st wagon.

Royal Talent

British King George VI enjoyed needlework and once made a dozen embroidered chair covers.

The High Life

A Greek monk, Simeon Stylites (right), spent 45 years preaching from the top of a 22-m high pillar.

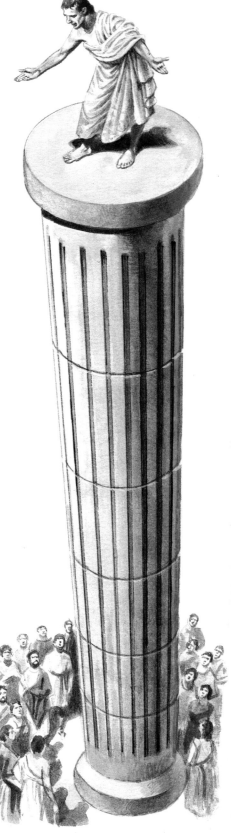

Musical Accomplishments

◆ *The longest of commonly performed operas is* Die Meistersinger von Nürnberg *by Richard Wagner (left) who, it is said, used to compose wearing fancy dress.*

◆ *In 1985, with equipment of his own invention, British eccentric Rory Blackwell from Devon played 108 different instruments simultaneously.*

◆ *The Italian castrato, Farinelli, could sing 8 notes above the normal human register.*

An Understanding Man

Dr Harold Williams spoke 58 languages and many dialects fluently. His attendance at the League of Nations in Geneva was invaluable as he was able to converse with every delegate in their own language.

Military

❖

Stephen Southernwood exactly dated the outbreak of the Second World War in a book published 8 years earlier.

❖

In January 1795, the French cavalry captured the entire Dutch fleet by surrounding the ships on the frozen Zuider Zee.

❖

Mohammed Ali, once ruler of Egypt, created two infantry regiments manned entirely by one-eyed soldiers.

❖

Robert E Lee, American Civil War soldier, is probably the only general to be offered command of both opposing forces in any war.

Dead Wood

German poet Hans von Thummel chose to be buried in the heart of an oak tree (below).

Fast Track

Mensen Ernst, a Norwegian cross-country runner, ran from Paris to Moscow, a distance of some 2800km, in only 2 weeks. He managed to run an average of 200km each day, despite having to swim 13 large rivers on the way.

How Low Can You Go?

Dennis Walston, alias King Limbo, slithered under a flaming bar only 15.25cm high on 2 March 1991, in Washington State, USA. The record for a performer on roller skates is 11.94cm, achieved by Syamala Gowri, aged 5, on 10 May 1993, in Andhra Pradesh, India.

Tapping Feat

The fastest rate ever measured for tap dancing is 32 taps per second by British dancer Stephen Gare of Sutton Coldfield in 1990. This works out at 1920 taps per minute — if he could keep going for as long as that.

The World Of Espionage

Legendary Spies

Supergrass
Over 17 years, US citizen John Walker supplied the Soviets with 1 million US Navy messages.

Caught Snapping
When he was shot down by the Soviets, US pilot Gary Powers (left) was flying a top secret spy aircraft, the U-2, which flew at an incredible altitude of 24,380m.

English Lies
For years, Anthony Blunt, advisor on paintings to Britain's Queen Elizabeth II, spied for the Russians.

Russian Tales
Soviet KGB agent Kalugin kept all his country's secrets until the Cold War ended. Then he spilled everything to the world in a sensational book called Spymaster.

Fashion Victim
When spy beauty Mata Hari (above) — spy for the Germans — was sentenced to death by firing squad, she demanded a new suit and pair of white gloves.

Intelligence Men
Novelists Compton Mackenzie, William Somerset Maugham, John le Carré and Graham Greene all worked for the British Secret Service at some point in their lives.

Frogman Spy
When diver Buster Crabb (below) disappeared, it was rumoured that he had been caught checking the underside of a Soviet warship — and eliminated.

War Moves
The US did not develop a coordinated foreign intelligence policy until 1941, after the disastrous Japanese aircraft attack on Pearl Harbour.

Tricks Of The Trade

Computers emit weak radio signals, which means spies can tap them for secret information.

Spies can install miniature cameras in photocopiers to photograph documents.

Security services tap 35,000 telephone lines in Britain every year.

MI6 tapped Soviet military phones from a tunnel beneath Berlin.

Scout's Honour
Robert Baden Powell, founder of the Boy Scout movement, was a British spy during the Boer War.

Spy Mistress
Stella Rimington (below), former director general of MI5, was the first woman to head an intelligence agency in the Western world.

Holy Smokescreen!
According to the Bible, in 1200BC the prophet Moses and the Jewish commander Joshua were both using spies.

Aerial Espionage

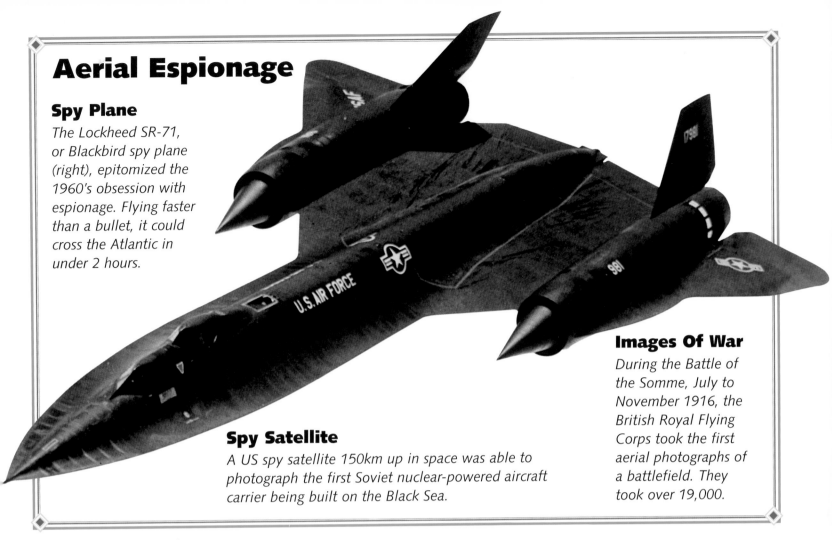

Spy Plane
The Lockheed SR-71, or Blackbird spy plane (right), epitomized the 1960's obsession with espionage. Flying faster than a bullet, it could cross the Atlantic in under 2 hours.

Images Of War
During the Battle of the Somme, July to November 1916, the British Royal Flying Corps took the first aerial photographs of a battlefield. They took over 19,000.

Spy Satellite
A US spy satellite 150km up in space was able to photograph the first Soviet nuclear-powered aircraft carrier being built on the Black Sea.

Secret Files
After the collapse of the Communist bloc in Eastern Europe and the end of the Cold War, it was discovered that the East German secret service had kept files on almost every person in the country.

Secret Agents
In the 10 years leading up to German reunification, the East German security service had at least 20,000 secret agents on the ground in West Germany waiting to go into operation if war broke out.

Codes And Ciphers

- ◆ During the Indian Mutiny, the British sent secret messages (left) written with invisible ink — a mixture of milk and lemon juice.

- ◆ The willow pattern on Chinese porcelain developed from a secret communications system in Ancient China.

- ◆ Morse Code translates the letters of the alphabet into dots and dashes, which can be tapped out or flashed by lights to convey information secretly.

- ◆ Julius Caesar, Charlemagne, Alfred the Great, Geoffrey Chaucer, Samuel Pepys, Mary Queen of Scots and Louis XIV all used codes or ciphers.

- ◆ Normans on the 1095 Crusade sent coded secrets by pigeon.

- ◆ The Navajo language was successfully used as a code by the USA in World War II.

Religion, Myth And Legend

Faith And Church

Ark-building

Noah's Ark (below) is said in the Bible to have measured 300 cubits in length, or 137m. By comparison, the longest royal yacht in the world, at 147m, is only slightly longer.

Every Sunday

Otto Brechel went to Sunday school every Sunday for 88 years (4576 times).

Record Sales

The Bible is the world's all-time bestselling book, and the most widely distributed.

Biggest Temple

Angkor Wat, Cambodia, is the world's biggest temple. The walls are 1550 x 1400m long.

Smallest Church

A chapel in Spain dedicated to Christopher Columbus is just 1.96sq m.

Ghost Ship

The *Flying Dutchman*, a phantom ship, was a bad omen for sailors who thought they saw it.

UFO-spotting

Some researchers say you are more likely to spot a UFO when Mars and the Earth are close together.

Birdmen

In one religious festival, Aztec warriors in Mexico used to dress like birds and jump off the top of high poles. They 'flew' down tied to long ropes.

Royal Cure

In 17th-century England, people believed that the touch of the king could cure diseases. King Charles II alone 'touched' 100,000 people.

Saints

❖

Ireland's St Patrick is thought to have been born in Wales and taken to Ireland by pirates.

❖

Of the 2000 registered saints, two-thirds are either French or Italian.

❖

The Catherine wheel firework is named after St Catherine of Siena, who was tortured on a spiked wheel.

❖

Comedians, dentists and gravediggers all have their own patron saint.

All-seeing Eye

The bows of ancient ships were given 'eyes' (right) for good luck and to guide the ship home safely.

Flowering

The first hyacinth is said to have grown from the blood of the mythical Greek youth Hyacinthus.

Vows Of Silence

Until the 1960's, Trappist monks kept vows of silence.

Sink Or Swim

In 17th-century England and America, the ability to float or swim was thought to be a sign that the person was a witch.

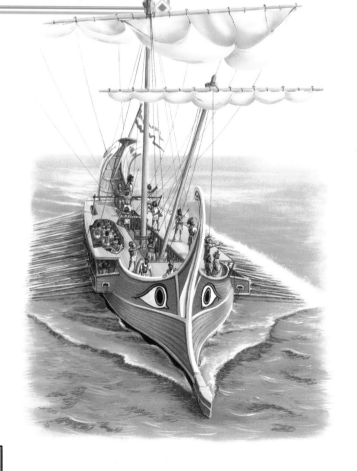

Starstruck

Western astronomers thought they were the first to discover the star Sirius B. It was later revealed that the Dogon people (right) of Mali, northwest Africa, had already worshipped Sirius B for centuries.

Echoing

The word 'echo' comes from the name of a nymph condemned in Greek mythology to speak only in reply.

Panic-stricken

The word 'panic' is derived from the name of the Greek god Pan. Legend says that he frightened travellers by jumping out at them in lonely places.

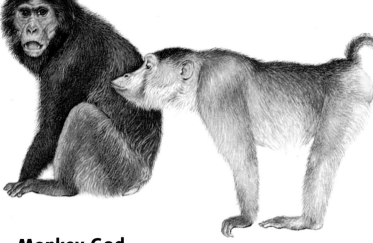

Monkey God

Hanuman is the Hindu monkey god. Although monkeys (above) often damage precious crops, farmers in certain parts of India leave them unharmed because of their resemblance to Hanuman.

No Bones About It

"Dragons' bones" form a cave near Beijing, China, were discovered to be 500,000-year-old human bones. The bones had been used to make pills.

Fire Chief

The Roman Emperor Nero is said to have played the fiddle while Rome burned. In fact, he rushed into the city to direct the fire brigade.

Beetle Worship

Dung beetles (left) were revered by the Ancient Egyptians, who considered them lucky. The beetles' habit of rolling dung balls to their nests reminded the Egyptians of the Sun-god Ra rolling the Sun across the sky every day.

Celestial Damp

The Ancient Romans used to offer sacrifices (below) to many gods, major and minor. Among them was the minor god Robigus, who was the god of mildew.

Big Swindles

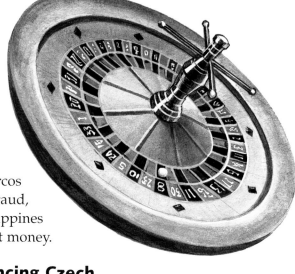

Bank Fraud

Alves Reiss conned the Bank of Portugal into printing bank notes for his use worth a staggering £1 million.

❖

In 1989, Italy's Banca Nazionale del Lavoro was defrauded of $5 billion.

❖

During the 2nd World War, the Germans used 140 Jewish prisoners to coin £130 million in counterfeit British currency.

❖

In 1873, 4 American financiers joined forces to swindle the Bank of England out of £102,000, They used convincing fake bills of exchange.

Wired To Win

Three electronics experts cheated at roulette (right) by sending remote-control signals to a bugged ball.

Fraudulent Fortune

Following reports that President Marcos had won the 1986 election through fraud, he and his wife (below) fled the Philippines — with $860.8 million of government money.

Bouncing Czech

In 1925, Czech-born Victor Lustig 'sold' the Eiffel Tower for scrap metal — twice!

Playing The Goat

Bogus 'Doc' Brinkley set up a hospital in Milford, Kansas, USA, in 1917 to implant goat glands into male patients to revive their sexual prowess.

Double Dupe

In 1983, both *Time* magazine and *Der Stern* published Hitler's diaries. The diaries were later found to be forgeries.

Monkey Business

Celebrated American showman P. T. Barnum charged people to see a man-eating chicken. The poor suckers saw just that — a man eating a chicken leg! He also displayed a mermaid (in fact a monkey and a fish glued together), and a wizened old lady, whom he claimed was aged 161. She was exposed as a hoax after her death.

Animal Swindles

◆ An EEC subsidy for transporting cattle between Northern Ireland and the Irish Republic encouraged one farmer during the 1970's to move his stock daily (below).

◆ Horatio Bottomley fixed a 6-horse race to finish in a certain order. His plans came to nothing when thick fog prevented the jockeys from being able to see each other.

◆ Two horses raced under false names in the 1844 Derby. The fraud was only discovered because there was an inquiry after one kicked the other.

◆ In 1945, all the greyhounds in a race but 1 were drugged. Instead of making them faster, the drug seemed to make them drunk — allowing the sober dog to win!

Fakes And Forgeries

Man Of Letters

Clifford Irving used forged letters to convince a publisher he was ghost writing the 'autobiography' of millionaire recluse Howard Hughes.

Wrong Note

Austrian-born violinist Fritz Kreisler (left) attributed many of the works he performed to 17th- and 18th-century masters, when he had in fact composed them himself.

Far-sighted

The Third Eye, a book about life in Tibet, was written by the Lama Lobsang Rampa, known to neighbours in Surrey, England, as Cyril Hoskins.

Divine Inspiration

Tom Keating (above) fooled art experts for 30 years with forged pictures 'inspired' by many great artists.

False Turning

The Vinland Map, which proved the Vikings had explored the New World, fetched $1 million when it was first discovered. Some 10,000 copies were sold for $15 before it was proved to be a fake.

False Smile

When the Mona Lisa was stolen in 1911, 6 Americans each paid £3 million for 'the real thing'.

Early Birds

Even in 246BC conmen were 'ageing' and selling manuscripts to collectors as antiques.

Fake Dome

The church of St Ignazio in Rome has a vast dome, but it can only be seen from the inside! Money ran out for the real thing in 1691, so a fake dome was painted on the flat ceiling.

House To Let

Arthur Ferguson conned $1 million dollars out of a trusting Texan when he 'leased' him the White House, Washington D.C., for a year. He convinced him that the US administration was trying to cut costs.

Spy Duped By Germans

During the 2nd World War, Turkish valet Elyesa Bazna (code-named 'Cicero') stole 52 top-secret documents from the British Ambassador and sold them to the Germans for £300,000. It was only after the war that he discovered the money he had been payed was forged.

Pirate Ahoy!

In 1921, Oscar Hartzell offered any descendants of Sir Francis Drake (left) the chance to claim a vast inheritance. He collected contributions from them for his legal fees and was never seen again!

Index